Songs from the Heart

by DiLaKool

Songs that come straight from the heart. Songs come from where and how life's road has been through a life time. Real heart felt. Life has a road that you have travel. You have to make it or it will take you. Live life that GOD sent you to live.

The contents of this work including, but not limited to, the accuracy of events, people, and places depicted; opinions expressed; permission to use previously published materials included; and any advice given or actions advocated are solely the responsibility of the author, who assumes all liability for said work and indemnifies the publisher against any claims stemming from publication of the work.

All Rights Reserved
Copyright © 2024 by DiLaKool

No part of this book may be reproduced or transmitted, downloaded, distributed, reverse engineered, or stored in or introduced into any information storage and retrieval system, in any form or by any means, including photocopying and recording, whether electronic or mechanical, now known or hereinafter invented without permission in writing from the publisher.

RoseDog Books
585 Alpha Drive
Suite 103
Pittsburgh, PA 15238
Visit our website at www.rosedogbookstore.com

ISBN: 979-8-89211-310-6
eISBN: 979-8-89211-808-8

Introduction

Hello, my name is Diana Baldwin.

I would like to tell everyone a little about me.

I grew up in a small town called Chilhowie, Virgina, land of many deer.

I knew everyone in the county. My family was a large family who was very musically talented. Extremely GODLY folks. I hold my values high in my Salvation.

I grew up early, having to be an adult as a child.

It just taught me to be a strong-willed, self-sufficient, to make a friend with everyone I come in contact with.

I have three brothers, one sister. My mother has always been my rock.

I graduated high school and trade school. I was educated by my dad in surviving, hunting, fishing, working in woodwork, cars, art, music, and law enforcement.

Though my dad wasn't in my life very much, I did learn a lot from him.

I got married as soon as I got out of school. I had plans of going into the Air Force, which I should have done. I guess we learn from our mistakes. Being married for thirty-some years, I found he had his own life going on. That was the day everything changed. I put on me again. I brought out the person I am.

I began to write, going to see my music that I knew was the biggest part of who I am.

I met up with Gene Odom, who was Ronnie VanZant's best friend and security on the plane crash of LYNYRD SKYNYRD.

The same time I met the PREACHER STONE BAND, who took me right under their wings. That was a dream come true. I'm finally part of a very famous band.

I have been working and traveling with both Gene Odom and the Band ever since. This has brought me to many friends around the world.

I have found what I love to do, meeting two of the most famous to most loving and caring people in my life.

Now while not with the band and my best friend, Gene Odom, you'll find me running a business, Baldwin's Heating & A/C, or full-time Arby's.

I love working with other bands and helping them sell merch and getting them shows. Finding myself overwhelmed by having someone believe in my writing.

This has been my dream all my life, to sing, write, and let people know there are still good people in the world that can make someone like me believe.

Follow your dreams.

By the River

Walking by the riverside,
Wondering if it's wrong or right.
Hearing the sound go by,
Wishing I didn't feel this inside.

While walking,
While walking,
Down by the riverside, feeling the joy, joy inside.

I could hear him call my name,
Walking by the riverside.
I know I'll feel the same,
Lifting me up to the mountaintop.
My Savior is one who never stops.
He'll carry me all the way, even on my good days.

While walking...
While walking...
Down by the riverside...
Feeling deep inside that joy, joy that abides.

I felt my LORD by my side,
The one who abides.
Walking by the riverside...
While... walking by the riverside...

This Time of Year

It's time that great changes come.
When the beauty of summer has been left behind,
Now winter will arrive.
The leaves have all fallen to the ground,
While everything is bare.

This time of year brings some sad, some cheer.
It can be a lonely time of year.

Don't know what to expect, great or small.
I'll face them all.

This time of year brings some sad, some cheer.
It can be a lonely time of year.

Lying beneath the snow lies beautiful things to grow.

Waiting to give life that glows.
Come forth, the LORD does say.
It's my gift from all the cold.
Now it won't be long.
This time of year brings some sad, some cheer.
It can be lonely time of year.
Lonely time of year.

Angels

They come from nowhere at all.
In the day or in the night.
They appear anywhere,
When you least know.
They all have a story, and to guide you everywhere you go.
They can be anyone at all.
Angels great and small.
Just when you feel so alone, when you hear that voice call,
They stand by your side, just waiting for you to need someone strong.
Don't be afraid when you hear one of them call,
Christ gave one to you or a legion if you call.
Angels to watch so you do not fall, or if you do they'll catch you.

Way You Feel

Open up my eyes,
They're the only ones who cry.
Open up my eyes.
Don't look inside.

The pain I feel, the hurt that cuts.
Nothing can bring you back from that.

I found your smile,
I found your love.
Nothing can change what I feel, not even from above.
The time we have,
We live it too fast.

Open up my eyes,
So I can see.
You're the one who belongs to me,
The one to make my dream.
Life of you and me.

Open up my eyes; they're the only ones who cry.
Open up my eyes, don't look inside.

Open up my eyes,
Don't look inside.
Don't...
Look inside...

I Run, I Run for Life

She was a young girl with big dreams.
She was so delightful,
Always a shining queen.

Being full of energy would take her away.
So smart and so sweet.
Living in a world of terror and things a child should not see.

The one who reaches for the stars and the moon.
The girl of life had no clue.
One day she will find what's true.
Not only the sun and the moon, there's also millions of stars too.
The life of being free and chasing her dream.

I run, I run for life...
For all that is free... for all that is free... like me...

Long Way Home

It started on the long road home.
No one I knew as the train rolled on.
Sailing like a ship in the night,
Was I doing this right?
The sound of rails as the sequel from the fast-
Running train.

Ride on… ride on…
Ride this train home.
Ride on… ride on…
Going to make it home.

The sun started rising as I wiped my eyes.
To a new day that had come, after a long ride on a midnight train.
I looked in the front, I looked in the back.
A train is like life, a one-way track.

My heart had been so far this time, I sure hope it's not been left behind.
The one I loved is so long passed,
No thinking of you at last.
I can hear you as you said, the train is coming not to be late.

Ride on… ride on…
Ride on… ride on…
Your girl is no longer to be by your side.
Ride on… ride on…
I wiped the tears from my eyes,
As I saw him as I went by.
She just waved as the train went by,
Ride on… ride on…
Ride on… ride on…

His Hand

I was lost out in the sea,
No one around be me.
I could feel my body weak,
Praying for my soul to keep.
I saw no hope in sight,
Nor could I see a light.
I closed my eyes and then I could see,
The LORD was holding me.
I could hear him as he spoke,
Don't worry, child, you will float.
I felt the warm blood running in my soul.
Not one ounce of cold.
Out of nowhere a light appeared,
A voice calling, over here.
I knew at once my LORD sent me the light that's within.
I tell the story not for just me, but for all to see,
The light that will guide thee.

Standing in the Rain

When I found what you've done to me,
I lost my mind, I lost my dream.
You cut me like a sword, the love I had I have no more.
I ran to get away from all the words you said.
They never meant a thing.
I heard the midnight train, I knew I was about to board.
The rain running down my face, listening as the engine raced down the tracks.
I could feel my heart as it broke, feeling like I was going to choke.
At once I knew I never meant nothing to you.
You had your other love, you always knew they were your true.
When the train arrived, finally I realized it, the tears running down my face, more than rain could ever make.
I got on board knowing nothing I was looking for from all the pain.
Now that I can be the only one to see, that there was never no love for me.
The midnight rain was not the same, it was all the tears I cried.
Now my eyes have dried to realize that I was dead for a long time.
I'll never go back, this is a one-way track.
You're free to be the one you was meant to be.
You surely was not the one for me,
You don't even have a clue of who I can be.
You chose the ones who you love, I'm not yours anymore.
I never was before. I'm not the joke, it's all on you.
Your love make-believe, there was never no you-and-me.
Going to ride the midnight train, till there's no more rain.
Going to keep on this train.

Home Again

I was just a child living in a grownup world.
Being Mom's little girl, while helping her to cope with
Things unknown.
Living to help my brothers and me to just be happy as could be.
Never once to complain, living so insane.
I always knew what to do, watching after them two.
Babies is what we were, but not much ever disturbed the love of the world.
The day came when it was time to go, it was hard to let Mom go.
I never knew how life would be, till the day he was caught cheating on me.
That's when all the memories came back, he's just like my dad.
I brought it all to light, boy, was that a fight.
No man likes to be made known of what is his own.
No identity for himself, using me to gain him love.
The lies he has and carries around
Makes him a boy in this town.
No man with a wife would cut her so low, a real man would let he go.
The jealousy that he has of his son, he uses her for his upkeep, to be a slave
till his grave.
Never will he give them up, nor take it to own.
I give him up to love no more, he's just a liar waiting to score from one more
whore, that he's keep from long before.
I will come to my home, it was never his to start.
He was never here or did his part.
The day will come to take his last breath.
I hope he prayed for HEAVEN to rest.
Home again, is where I'll be. It's my place and there I'll be.

Your Eyes

Open your eyes so you can see,
There's no man left inside of me.
I walked the straight and narrow way,
Just to find out it had to be your way every day.

I packed my gear without one doubt.
Close that door behind me so you can't see out.
My shadow will be all that is left,
Walking into the sunset.

Going to find my dream I've waited for all my life.
Giving up things just to make it right.
I'll never look back 'cause there's only today.
I will be happy this way, no heart to share, not once of care.
This the point, nothing else to share.

It's so Cold

It's so cold, it's so cold, my heart is cracking to pieces.
The parts that can't be put together again.
I keep looking for a warm place to park.
A warm place for my heart.
No one to share, no one to care.
Nothing to bare but a frozen heart.
I love only as a friendly way,
No love can come that can stay.

Alone is not so bad, you see,
It holds my hand consistently.
It's only a frozen heart waiting for spring.
Waiting for the part of me that will bloom.

I'm not so frozen anymore,
The sunshine and now I feel warm.
Making everything inside and be able to sleep through the night.

It Just Is

The night was long, just one lonely song.
Playing in my head to repeat what is said,
Living in a crazy world.
I'm just one of the lonely girls, lonely for the music playing in my soul.
Wanting it more and more,
What more can be said?
Listing to the words people say,
Oh, ya, nothing what they claim.
Words are easy to say, but not when you play.
I hear what you say, it's not close to what you play.
Words are words with no love to show,
How can it ever grow?
Leaving it all behind to walk away,
Never more to hear you play.
I'm reaching for the stars now, shining down on the ground.
Walking by the moonlight, keeping you out of my sight.
Tap to the beat along the way, 'cause it has nothing to say.
Broken words and broken dreams, waking up to a new song to sing.
All new people, none from before,
I never knew till I was out the door. Keep your friends 'cause they're not mine,
That's your heart and you will find,
You played too much, now be left behind.
Walking on with this song of mine, now it's time for you to fall.
Feel the pain like falling rain, it will aways remain.
Feel it inside like a cutting knife, just one more slice.
It's okay, it will fade away.
Someday it will fade away.

I'm Closing the Door

I'm closing the door, there's too much pain,
Running very deep in my veins.
Every word was a lie and you knew,
It cut like a knife, leaving me to die.

No more hanging my head to cry,
I'm coming back strong,
Putting you where you belong.
There's nothing in you, not one bit of truth.
Your path seems cool, you run into this fool.
I'll break you down, stomp you in the ground.
There's no love to be found.
I'll walk every step of the way,
Just to make you feel this pain.
You fooled me once but you won't twice.
It's time for you to roll the dice, will you find it nice?

Don't turn your back, I'll be right there.
I'll be giving you back with a small crack.
There will be no more games to play,
You're not taking everything.

I'll take your heart down to the core,
You'll wish to see me no more.
It will be the last you know that you've got to go.
My last goodbye will cut you inside.
You will remember how you caused me pain.
No one to help you, no one to care.
The door has closed for you now too.
Don't feel so blue, it's you.
It's you...

It Was Something Crazy

Looking your way, you was looking mine.
Chilling with long-lost stuff.
Killing my love, killing my love.
Once wasn't enough,
Killing my love, killing my love.

Flying through, everything we do.
I look in your eyes, nothing to see.
Your love has never been for me.
Taking what you can, saying anything to get what you need.
Leaving me to stand alone in every way.

Killing my love, killing my love.
Killing my love, killing my love.

Killing my love, killing my love.
Killing my love, killing my love.

I let go of the one who wanted me to,
But I stayed with you.
It was such a great mistake.
He tried giving his all, big and small.
Taking me straight to his heart,
Begging to never part, I had made his life complete.
Oh, what did he see in me, to love so strong?

Killing my love, killing my love. Killing my love, killing my love...

Give Me a Place

I got out of bed, with the sound of the guitar in my head.
The sound of the strings as each one rings, the most beautiful sound I've ever seen.
The old blue jeans, with t-shirt and flannel, I feel so fine.

Give me a place, I'll play all night.
Give me a reason and I might play two.
Give me my time, you'll love my rhymes.

I'll find a place and set down my case
To grab me a bite and think about the night.
I love the way they love me while I play,
But then it goes back to the same ol' thing.
Get up from the table and put on my coat.
Going to find me a new joint.
While driving in my truck, I think of a new song
One that no one has thought of at all.
I sing it over in my head, to be sure each word is said.

Give me a place, I'll play all night.
Give me a reason and I might play two.
Give me time, you'll love my rhymes.
Let the music take you away, while you listen to me play.
It will take over your mind and soul, and you'll be listening to every word.
Seeing the man that knows how you play.
Don't give a damn and stands for what he plays.
It's so captivating that you're in my control.
This man playing and taking your soul,
It's been an awesome show and downright tonight.
While packing up, people come by, boy, you know how to put on a show.
Slowly I walk out to my ride, to drive off for another night.

You Just Never Knew

As you walked down the hill,
No one could tell what new was to come.
The look in your eyes I saw,
A man full of life to bring.
Songs in his heart and ready to sing.
Fingers of gold, that will unfold and make the music ring.

You just never knew what you could mean.
You just never knew, I knew everything was not from your heart.
The lips don't speak of truth,
Just things you hide inside.

Broken from pieces from your lies,
When you was known as the best.
You let it all slip away because you choose to play the
Wrong way.
You just never knew no more love for you,
'Cause it all slipped away, you just never knew.
You just never knew 'cause you choose too.

You Took My Song

You took my song and you took me,
Along you told me everything that you wanted me to hear.
It didn't take me too long to really catch on.
I seen things you've been doing behind my back now.
The things you said, was it true, you know they're really lies.
I still believed your lies.
I knew from the beginning, so why can't you tell me, baby?
Because you know it's going to hurt you so.
You can't keep going on, you'll never find a new song.
This one hurts and it cuts so deep, no one can get no sleep.
Why couldn't you tell me, baby?
Why did you have to tell me last?
You should have known, I was smarter than that.
But now you're in a trap.
You can never look back, it's a one-way track.
Everything I said was true, would have saved you a lot of heartache and pain.
I'm going to take it away,
Oh, yes, I'm going to take it away.
I'm going to take it away,
Take it away
Take away

Hold On

I was tired and ready to go wherever I roam.
Leaving this place I've always called home.
The days have grown cold, no family of my own.
Looking for somewhere to belong.

Hold on… hold on…
Hold on… hold on…

I've let this world go, it's too hard of a toll.
It's torn and ripped me apart, love had taken the beat.
I will leave it all behind maybe not too far from now.

Hold on… hold on….
Hold on… hold on…

I've given my best to make others' dreams come true,
But not feel the same for you.

I've given my all, to nothing is left,
So beating and grasping for air.

Hold on… hold on…
Hold on… hold on…

I've closed my eyes to see the man, who said he was there to take my hand.
He said no fear, I have you here,
The same as I've told you before.
I'll hold on and forevermore.

Hold on… hold on…
Hold on… hold on…
Hold on to the KING… hold on…
He's holding me while he carries me home…

Only in the Night

Only in the night,
Only in the night.
You can feel it watching,
You can feel it near.
Only in the night,
With a hungry bite.
You can run,
But you can't hide.
It knows where you are at all times,
Only in the night.
The fog is rising, the moon is full,
There's no paths as you run.
There's no time to lose, it's there watching you.
Only in the night.
Feeling full of fright, can't go left or right.
Everything is closing in, not one neighbor, not one friend.
Looking all around, you know it's going to end.

Only in the night...
Only in the night...

One Down

One down, two to go.
One night, one more show.
Look around, what do you see?
All the music surrounding me.
One down, two to go, it was a sold-out show.
Life is hard and life is deep, you just can't keep.
Hard to please and a lot less sleep, one more night to meet.
One down, two to go, one more night and one more show.

Kind Heart

Kind heart just causes pain.
It's taken like pouring rain.
They'll hurt you to get anything, not worrying about your
pain or the shame you've caused.

Kind heart leads to destruction to the rest of you.
Overtaking your brain, killing your heart while it's running through your
veins.
Promises that are to never come true.
That's what you do.
Let it control you and run like the wind.
Nothing lasts forever, I hate to break your style.
Just when you think it's the end,
That's when it really begins.
You can't hide your lying eyes, they tell the story that never tried.
I've overcome what was so deep.
Now I can lay my head to sleep.
Till morning comes I will not weep, only sleep.

Just Get Up and Go

I got up, ready to go. Got to find a new show.
I sling my guitar on my back. I'm ready to make tracks.
I live to play, with words to say.
I burn for the strings to ring, I feel my blood as it flows.
Only me and another show.
Listening to the crowd as they scream for more.
Don't stop playing, in my hands and mind,
There is no time.
I play deeper in soul, as I feel myself out of control.
Play it loud, play it hard.
Only time for one more song.
I feel as they slowly go, it's almost over, till the next show.

I pack up my gear, listening as I hear,
The music still rings in my ear.
Wonder what place he's from, he's really good, son.
They'll never know, he's on the go.
No time to stop, no place to stay.

This is just how he plays.
Longing for the day, he'll be more famous,
Everyone to say, I saw that guy one day.
The laughs and jokes that were once told
Became my living soul.
Not to giving an inch, to what they say,
I will not stop for my dream, I'm in for the real thing.

Only sleep for an hour or two, I have to stay on the move.
Music to play, words to sing.
Not letting no one put a stop to me.
Roll right through the night, finding that light.
That moves my life of fright.

Walking in I sat right up, knowing in my gut.
Shaking to get ahold of my guitar, that makes what I'm looking for.
No time to waste, no time to spare, playing is in the air.
The sound that takes you out of control,
Has now captured your soul.

Playing as the sweat rolls down my face.
Loving the feel of what's real
From my head to my toes.
One-man, one-man show.
The night has come to a close, as this man hits the road.
Playing where who knows, he'll be back for sure.
As walking into the night, he felt what was right.
The man with the plan, he was the man who can.
He was the man who can...

If I Could Imagine

If I could only see what you have made for me,
The beauty only you have made,
I've seen all you've done down here.
But that cannot compare to all the beauty up there.

I fell the love from day to day.
Like from the morning sun, the light is what brings life
Unto the night.
If I could only see,
What you have made for me.

Made with love for all to share,
Brings upon us kindness, not despair.
I sit and watch as the night slowly comes, with silence of darkness as the fog rolls in.

The moon peeks over the mountaintop, to give light for a small glimpse of what's to come.
The light to shine till the morning sun.

If only my eyes could see, the midnight is full of things.
No need to worry, no need to be scared.
It will be fine with nothing to fear, I know my LORD is near.
If only my eyes could see, it's okay to follow me.
I give my life to whom I proclaim,
I am his child with no fear, I know he'll take me there.
To the place I long to see, the streets of Heaven with my KING.
If I could only imagine what my eyes will see, walking along the riverside.
Singing songs with all that have gone.
Oh, what a day that will be, when my eyes get to see.
Oh, what a day that will be, when my eyes get to see....

I Miss You, My Child

I miss you, my child,
I miss that smile.
You are the light that
Shines so bright.

I miss you, my child,
I miss that smile.
I miss the calls I used
To always get.
I miss my boy that
Brings me joy.

Time has now flown by,
I carry these tears in my eyes.
I remember the day, you would say,
I love being here every day.

I've watched you grow, I'll never let you go.
You're a part of my soul.
It breaks me, to see the little boy living his dream.
I can't never say goodbye, it would break me inside.
I want you to know, as long as I'm alive
You'll always have love and a home to arrive.
You are my joy, the star in my eye.
I'II never say goodbye.
I love you always, my child,
Elijah Deshawn Lee Albertson.

Your Aunt DiLaKool

Oh It's Me

Oh it's me, oh it's me, oh it's me, oh it's me.
Standing in the midnight hour, looking all around, feeling like the power is coming from the ground.
Lighting flashing in the air, thunder rolling through the sky.
Tell me, oh, tell me which way to fly.
I get visions as I run through the woods,
Things that cut me and left to bleed.
The things you did to me.
Oh, look what you've done,
Oh, look what you've done.

You took me in and turned me upside down,
You ripped me to pieces, and you didn't give a damn.
The time is coming when you think you're set free,
Depends when you'll find out it's your turn to see.

All your body will be tortured, your heart turned to stone.
You'll be left to believe all the things,
That make you fear everything down here.
No more for you anymore, you had it all before.
Your lies took you for a ride, and took me for my things with your lies.
I could be in a better place, you see, you see what you have done.
Oh look, oh look what you have done for me,
You feel the pain that you see.
Time has come that I've thrown it all away.
Now you have to live with the pain you got every day.
The path you chose after what you said,
Will bring you misery.
It's yours to claim that your heart isn't mine.
It belongs to the love of your heart.

Oh, look what you see, oh, look what you see was what was your dream,
She makes you hers and you cannot leave.
It's your payment for games you play.
I said don't look back,
You're a bad memory.
I don't need your grief, I'm a shadow and a scar around your neck of what you really had.
Keep going with the one who's going to take it all,
Be ready for what's a great big fall.
Last call, here I come, listening to them call.
Fall... fall... fall... f...a...l...l...

Clouded Mind

It happened all at once, when I first saw you I was hooked.
I was shaking like a kid in love.
You sucked me in,
When you knew I was in pain.
You told me lies, while making me believe you was real.
To find you was just clouding my mind.

You sat me up, to think it was real, you took my all till there was no more.
I could feel my soul as it fell on the floor,
'Cause you told me you loved me no more.
You just clouded my mind.

Now I have nowhere to turn, no one to love and nothing to give.
Just a clouded mind.
No love, no games to play, you done took it all away.
You've left me with a clouded mind.
I'm walking far away, never more to hear you say,
Those things you do not mean, you're just a taker who'll never be seen.
The road you made is all of your own
When you find you've no home
Finding you have lost it all.

Don't Worry

Don't worry if you don't see me again,
I'll be in a better land, don't be sad.
I'll be singing beyond glad,
It's okay,
You never got to know me, for helping you all the time
Instead of leading a helping hand.
I'll be home in my promised land, don't worry if you don't see me again.
I'm just in a better land, with JESUS I'll stand.
No looking to the left, no looking to the right.
Just to know everything is alright.
So don't worry if you don't see me again,
Don't worry, I'm at home.

Songs from the Heart

I hope you like what I have sent.
This is some from off top of my head.
I have more, I would love to use them as poems also.
The best I have I'm working on getting them typed up.

I've waited so long to have this chance.
I have music but it's recorded as they come out in singing.

Sincerely, DiLAKool

You Took My Song

You took my song, you took me along, you told me everything you wanted me to hear.
It didn't take too long to really catch on, I seen the things you've been doing behind my back now.
The things you said, was it true, you know they're really lies, you know I knew from the beginning.
So why can't you tell me, baby?
I said why can't you tell me, baby?

You know it's going to hurt you so,
you can't keep going on, you'll never find another new song,
it will cut everyone so deep.
Why couldn't you tell me, baby, why did you have to tell me last?
You should have known that I was smarter than the other ones.
You can never look back,
I'm taking everything, it's going to hurt you.
Why couldn't you tell me lately everything I said was so true, it would have saved you a lot of heartache cuz I'm going to take it away.
Oh, yes, I'm going to take, oh, yes, I'm going take.
I'm going to take it all away,
take it all away...

Walking

I'll never walk on the highway, I'll only watch from afar.
The things I was running for have been gone for a while.
The words that are said are just to please your head, and make your heart think it's true.
When it was just words, that you use.
I hear them from others too so I know I'm not the only one.
You have many you give to. So don't look into my eyes to see,
that they is not you or me.
Your heart belongs to just one, you've said it over and over again,
so now you have won.
Don't call me yours, 'cause you know that I'm not.
You play only to get what you've got.
One day those words you say so well, will be the ones to kill you, the way you killed me each day.
I may be your fool for only a little while, but in my heart I knew you had more, it was for sure.
The things you said to me, I heard others say them too.
It could have others come from you.
I watch while you play with so many, so don't be surprised when you get so broken.
No one by your side, I'll be gone forever with nothing of me.
I tried my best when you was low, but then you let me go.
Your wish came true, so take it while you can, 'cause it won't last forever, you'll find yourself alone.
You've broken everything I thought that I had.
Your change of plans you had made
When you was living a double life, so don't be surprised when you have nothing by your side.
So don't be surprised when you have nothing by your side.

Time

The morning breaks and I find my day.
Beginning in a new way, a new place.
Holding on to nothing, and nothing new.

It all began with you,
and I don't know what to do.
Just close my eyes,
while tears fall all down my face.
No one place to be, that's me.

I pick a tune or two, to make my life begin,
To fill my day. I'm looking both ways.
I get a call for one more show,
Then where do I go?

It all began with you,
and I don't know what to do.
Just close my eyes,
while tears fall all down my face.
No one place to be, that's me.

There's no one place to be, that's me
That's me...

Running in the Night

Running in the night, knowing what's wrong or right
Fighting to keep my head on right, you tore my heart, you stripped me of my life,
thinking you was my light.
I can't take it anymore, no, not once more.
I have you, everything you stand for,
I loved you beyond the stars.
You have to cut me even more hard.
I've bled dry, I can't even cry.
I've erased the life from my heart, it's not yours anymore.
You can't have this man that you once swore to adore.
Instead you broke my heart, and messed with my head.
I'm placing you below, in a cold, dark hole,
Never to spread your evil soul.
I'll carry you no more.
I'm crazy in the head, that's what she really did.
I'm fighting to keep my life.
To reach what is right, my dream I once swore I'd never stop, to reach the top.
I have my love, that gives it all. Just can't ever give away the heat.
I gave it to the girl that will always be my world, because I need everything,
I won't let her go.
To make me look so, I can reach more, not just one the one.
I'll use the whole world
To make my dream and perform.

It's Me

It's me, oh it's me, oh it's me.
Standing in the midnight hour looking all around, feeling like the power is coming from the ground.
Lighting flashing in the air, thunder rolling through the sky.
Tell me, oh, tell me which way.
Oh tell me, oh tell me which way can I fly,
I get visions as I run through the woods.
So far of the things you did to me, that cuts me into the stone,
which left me to bleed.
You took me in and you turned me upside down, you ripped me to pieces and didn't give a damn.
Oh, look what you've done, oh, look what you've done to me.
Oh, look what you've done to me....

Like the Swift Sweeping Wind

Like the swift sweeping wind,
you showed up, it blew you right in.
You shined like the sun,
You glowed like gold.
Oh, but was your way, different in soul.

You're like a very sharp sword,
The eyes pierce you within.
The words you speak, you can totally captivate.
The voice so sweet and kind,
But really a lion behind,
Waiting for the kill.

Your spirit is strong and eager to grow, eager to fly, eager to shine.
The gift of what holds your soul.
The sound of music rips you whole.
Lift up your head to reach the sky,
While your hands just glide.
You have no mercy, you have no love, except for the music,
that's your dream, let the music ring.

You're like a very sharp sword,
The eyes pierce within.
The words you speak, you can totally captivate.
The voices so sweet and kind.
But really a lion behind,
Waiting for the kill.

Waiting for the kill,
Waiting for the kill.

Because We're Curious

Because we're curious to who folks were.
Became the way the Hell House to stay, if we hadn't been there that day.
The first sight the man did say, if we had not been there that day.
Through his mind was surely to play, is that Ronnie Vanzant standing up there I see?
Then we started walking down and they couldn't believe.
On that day history was made because of two people who stuck around to say, we know all about the Hell House and wish it could stay this way.
For little was known but this guy did say, he would buy this land, to keep it preserved.
He kept his every word,
every word he said, now gone way too soon, but to his word was true.
From far and wide people will know he tried. To keep it all alive until! he died way too soon.
The legend of the Hell House will live on in the ones who carry on.
Never forget what music has done and where it has brought us from.
Legends now to help carry the Lynyrd Skynyrd songs will on and on
play those songs, play those songs.

Changes

Changes,
Making changes,
Changes,
Making changes.

Nothing here, nothing nowhere.
Going to a place that I can
make changes.
The ones that help to make
the dark turn into light.

Changes,
Making changes,
Changes,
Making changes.

Every time I reach the top,
Someone tries to make me stop.
I've held on so tight that I
Can't anymore. Give me more.

Changes,
Making changes,
Changes,
Making changes.

How long can I go, how long
can I wait.
Only a few really knew.
I'm making changes.

Changes,
Making changes,
Changes,
Making changes.

So many that have bled me dry.
With no tears in my eyes
I will survive.
I'm making changes.

Changes.
Making changes,
Changes,
Making changes.

Changes...

I Lower My Head

I lower my head.
I give my best
I will do all I can
To stay true, and give out my light.

When walking away, into a new place
I feel your love all over me.
I can't help but shout and sing
Because you are my only King.

When I'm alone, you talk so long.
You know it helps keep me strong.
Nowhere I would rather be,
than in your presence, my only King.
Lift me up in my last day,
I want to hear my dear Lord say,
It's me, it's okay.
It's time to make your way.
Don't be worried, it's okay.

The Lord came for me,
To make my way
Make my way...

Why

Can you tell me why?
You made so much, then turned out into a lie.
Why?
You take what you can, that makes you feel like a man.
Who?
Can't you even hold up your head, your family turns you away.
Is this how you repay the one who gave up everything in every way?
Go leave, don't ever be seen, I just want to scream.
Hurt inside, fall to pieces over and over again in your nightmare.
I will watch you fall, not help you when you can do all is crawl.
Why?
'Cause you're a low-class guy with nothing but greed, thought we was a team.
I see right through what you and her do.
Not on your own neither deserve your home.
Why?
Your life went out of control, you're not a child so you can't go back home, so you give her your all, stabbing us all
While you live so fine, and you wine and dine with what you think is fine as gold.
Oh, and the one that you hold.
I'm finding the time, even you will give up your soul, then will you die growing old.
Finish up and die, in the web you have spun.
So long, it's all done.

www.ingramcontent.com/pod-product-compliance
Lightning Source LLC
LaVergne TN
LVHW010123170826
845678LV00012B/2566

* 9 7 9 8 8 9 2 1 1 3 1 0 6 *